KUSHTI IN BANARAS

Wrestling as a Homage to the Gods

To Bernard-Yves Sabot
well-known in Banaras as Dr Sab

Pahalwans believe that the earth of the *akhara's* pit is a sacred element. During fights, the mud smeared on the body helps wrestlers to strenghten their grip on their opponent's limbs, wet by perspiration.

KUSHTI IN BANARAS

Wrestling as a Homage to the Gods

Photographs

SÉVERINE DABADIE

Text

CHRISTIANE ETCHEZAHARRETA &
SÉVERINE DABADIE

Lustre Press
Roli Books

HANUMAN CHALISA

Jai Hanuman gyan gun sagar
Jai Kapis tihun lok ujagar

Victory to thee, O'Hanuman! Ocean of Wisdom - All hail to you O'Kapisa! (fountain-head of power,wisdom and Shiva-Shakti). You illuminate all the three worlds (entire cosmos) with your glory.

Ram doot atulit bal dhama
Anjani-putra Pavan sut nama

You are the divine messenger of Shri Ram. The repository of immeasurable strength, though known only as son of Pavan (wind), born of Anjani.

Mahavir Vikram Bajrangi
Kumati nivar sumati Ke sangi

With limbs as sturdy as *vajra* (the mace of God Indra) you are valiant and brave. On you attends good sense and wisdom. You dispel the darkness of evil thoughts.

Kanchan varan viraj subesa
Kanan kundal kunchit kesa

Your physique is beautiful, golden coloured, and your dress is pretty. You wear earrings and have long curly hair

Hath vajra aur dhuvaje viraje
Kandhe moonj janehu sajai

You carry in your hand a lightening bolt along with victory (*kesari*) flag and wear the sacred thread on your shoulder.

Sankar suvan kesri nandan
Tej pratap maha jag vandan

As a descendant of Lord Sankar, you are a comfort and pride of Shri Kesari. With the lustre of your vast sway, you are propitiated all over the universe.

Lord Hanuman is worshipped by the *pahalwans* as the epitome of power, valour, and strength; important values in the practice of *kushti*.

Facing page: A sailing boat on the River Ganges near the Chet Singh palace.

'What is an akhara? It is a place of recreation for youth. It is a shrine of strength where earth is turned into gold. It is a sign of masculinity and the assembly hall of invigorated youth. Strength is measured against strength and moves and counter moves are born and developed. An akhara should be in an open area where fresh air and sunshine mingle. It should be away from dirt and filth and in a place where the earth is soft. It should be set off by a boundary of some sort and surrounded by thick foliated trees. There should be water nearby. One should enter the akhara after paying obeisance and offering up incense to the Lord. An akhara is where one prays and where offerings are given and distributed. Its earth is saluted and taken up to anoint one's shoulders and head. And then one wrestles and the sound of slapping thighs and pounding chests fills the air. Grunts and groans of exertion echo ominously. One trounces and in turn is trounced. Exercise is done. Laziness and procrastination are drowned in sweat. The earth is mixed and finally one salutes the pit and leaves.'

- S. Alter, Joseph, 'Ratan Patodi, 1973' in
'The Wrestler's Body: Identity and Ideology in North India', 1992.

In the remarks of this former wrestler, all is said and all still remains to be said. The world of wrestling is a world apart – out of time, out of reality.

In the unbearable heat of the month of June, Banaras was plunged into an overpowering torpor. The first vision of the *akhara* (sports ground) of Gaya Seth seemed unreal. Wrestlers (*pahalwans*), covered with mud, with projecting muscles and proud breasts were sitting on a shaded square on the ground. An old man lying down in the centre, shared their intimacy. Bathed in an ochre light, they were oscillating between the creation and the end of the world. A new age, an unreal space.

The wrestling fraternity is closely knit by virtues of bravery and valour. It transcends all social differences of its people. The loyalty that unites the wrestlers surpasses all other relationships among sportsmen.

Wrestling in India, and particularly in Banaras, goes back to ancient times. A certain form of wrestling was practised before the one brought by the Mughals in the eleventh century: Bharatiya *kushti* (Indian wrestling) or simply *kushti*, as it is called.

In this country where religion impregnates each act of everyday life, *kushti* has blurred the religious borders, just as music has done. Even though the Mughals brought it as a strong print of their identity, Hindus adapted to it by introducing religious rituals into it and dedicating the sport to the deities of their pantheon.

Indian wrestling is also a way of ascetic living, implying not only intensive physical training, but also a

Painting decorations of the snake of Lord Shiva on a *rickshaw*.

Facing page: A brahmin *murti walla* (idol maker) during Durga Puja.

A marriage ceremony; the father of the girl performs *kanya daan* in Hindu weddings.

Facing page: Prayers held at Sultan Keshwara, a village in the Dashashvamedh ghat, during Maha Shivratri.

नूरी

A funeral procession in Manikarnika ghat.

Facing page: A lady performing funeral rituals near the holy fire at Manikarnika ghat.

At Gaya Seth *akhara*, the old tradition of giving lessons under a tree continues. Even though the guru is held in extremely high esteem by the wrestlers, a warm friendship unifies them.

code of ethics, personal hygiene and specific diet, celibacy, sexual abstinence, devotion, discipline and a multitude of other moral values. This unique sport requires a balancing of the body and spirit – it is a worship offered to the deepest human values, to the world of gods, to an ideal. *Kushti*, has something to do with the search of the ideal, a harmony between human beings and gods. 'Every wrestler continues to improve until he has pierced the sky,' said the Pandit of Ram Singh's *akhara*, where numerous champions have received training.

Traditionally, wrestlers were *brahmacharis* and they had to live with their spiritual teacher. Brahmacharya is the ancient practice of strict celibacy, a life of moral restraint, and dedication to one's education, which in this case implies the art of wrestling. According to custom and belief, only those men who can control their semen can become true wrestlers. Nowadays, in a modern setup, this ideal is difficult to follow and thus very rare. Under family pressure many wrestlers get married and take on the responsibility of raising a family. The inevitable fallout is that they are able to come to the *akhara* less frequently.

Generally, the practice of wrestling is a family tradition. Boys start wrestling at the age of seven or eight years and most wrestlers are teenagers or young men in their early twenties. Often wrestlers choose to practise *kushti* in an *akhara* nearest to their residence.

Wrestlers belong to different economic backgrounds and social status but in the daily life of an *akhara* these differences are not important. Around fifty per cent of the wrestlers in Banaras are Yadavs (the milkmen caste); twenty per cent are Thakurs; and about fifteen per cent are Brahmins, while the rest belong to a wide range of caste groups like Dhobis, Chandals, Chamars, Nayees, etc.

A typical wrestler hopes to join the army, the police, or the railways but most of the older wrestlers are not as educated as the younger ones. While some wrestlers retire and open tea stalls, many of them do business or are in government service, especially in the railways. In Banaras, many wrestlers work in the famous factory of Diesel Locomotive Works (DLW), where too stands a famous *akhara*.[1]

All *akharas* do not resemble each other and many, it should be said, have lost the essence of their true identity. Some of them have managed to slip through time without being spoiled by the perverse influence of modernity; they are true temples, where men and gods get together in a wonderful play.

While there are a few *akharas* where Muslims and Hindus practise together, there are many more in which segregation along communal lines is the norm. Although we didn't pose this question in the Gaya Seth *akhara*, the Hindu character of the place seemed predominant. Some *akharas* in Banaras are exclusively Muslim as well. The Mazdoor Health Improvement Association, established in 1931 to foster ideals of physical fitness and national self-determination among *mazdoors* (wage labourers), is located down a small lane in Madanpura. The association is almost entirely Muslim and most of the members come from the neighbourhood of a mosque called Al'lu ka Masjid.

A 'Guruji' directs an *akhara*, dictates its rules. He is the backbone of the place. He defines the objectives and sanctions if they are needed. In addition to his role as coach, he is the leader of the *akhara*.[2] When he crosses the threshold of the *akhara*, each one of the wrestlers comes to greet him and touch his feet in deference. He is admired, feared, and venerated as the master but he can always listen to everyone.

In general, former champions naturally go on to become a Guruji. In Gaya Seth *akhara*, Manohar Pahalwan won the bronze medal in the world championship of wrestling

Not merely rope-climbing, this daily exercise is a test of flexibility and manoeuvring skill. *Akharas* in Banaras provide traditional forms of training even in present times.

1 A substantial part of this information has been obtained from the excellent study by Joseph Alter in *The Wrestler's Body: Identity and Ideology in North India* (Berkeley: University of California Press, 1992).

2 'The 'Guruji' manages the *akhara*. He instructs his disciples on the fine art of wrestling. He prescribes each wrestler's individual regimen by delineating the number and sequence of exercises, the types and number of moves to be practised, the content and quantity of diet, and the time and amount of rest. The Guruji is also a source of strength and wisdom. . . . Many *akharas* have a shrine dedicated to the founding guru.' Joseph Alter, ibid.

during the Eighties and competed in international matches a number of times. But *kushti* training can also be a family tradition. At Bara Ganesh, for example, Lallu Pahalwan was the fifth-generation lineal guru of his *akhara*.

More than any other Indian sport, *kushti* is framed by many rites. Each day at dawn, the wrestlers come to pay homage to Lord Hanuman. Before the shrine of the highly venerated monkey-god, they bow reciting the mantras dedicated to him. After warming up, they gather before the pit (*akhara*), their palms joined in front of their chest. A few of them hold an incense stick and sometimes, flower petals are thrown on the pit creating a delicate colourful carpet. Then they chant together: *'Ram ki jay, Hanuman ki jay, Guruji ki jay.'*

Daily, the wrestlers warm-up with the same exercises: deep knee bends (*baithak*), jack knifing push-ups (*dands*) and rope climbing (*ras*). These exercises are endlessly repeated like mantras, in order to begin moving the body – which is more than just a physical routine – in a perpetual movement that becomes a kind of meditation. The body and the spirit come together in the same effort and breath.

A rope comes down from a branch of the majestic banyan. The climbing men follow one another; with powerful and sculptural muscles, the wrestlers rise towards the sky, taking the help of their arms alone, competing with each other. Some are training together time after time, in a tireless way, graving each other. These exercises must have become automatic for them. The bodies of the contenders have to be recognised, held and unbalanced, in order to make them fall. This is a game where skill, strength, equilibrium and force are the qualities needed by the wrestlers. They have two symbolic gears belonging to them – the *gadas* and the *joris* – maces that they whirl in

Famous wrestler, Ganga Pahalwan, with his name written in Urdu in the backdrop. Hindus and Muslims have been associated with the same passion — *kushti* — for many years. Like the representations of Hanuman, Muslims too proudly carry the *gada*.

The late Baba Biru Das, who was the resident sadhu of Gaya Seth *akhara*. As the priest of the *akhara*, it is a sadhu's duty to honour Hanuman and sanctify this holy place by his presence and prayers.

front of and behind themselves, whose weight can reach more than sixty kilograms.

Lord Hanuman is always depicted with a *gada* in the left hand. The old photographs of wrestlers often show them with a *gada*, making them look like gods of modern times. It is the emblem of any wrestler. For practising and exercising, they also use a large circular stone, hollowed in its centre with an axle grip which allows it to be seized and risen, known as the *nal*.

After the warm-up, the wrestlers head towards the *akhara*. Before entering, each wrestler touches it with the tip of his fingers and puts the dust on his forehead as a sign of veneration, because this ground is considered holy. A standing statue of Lord Hanuman inside an alcove watches over the events. He is painted orange-red, which is the characteristic colour of Sankat Mochan, the Redeemer. This explains the colour of the *langot* (loincloth) worn by the wrestlers, which is mostly red.

Inside the pit, the *pahalwans* stand face to face and stare at each other in a challenging manner. They clap their hands on their thighs, a traditional sign announcing the attack. The confrontation begins. They clutch each other with their arms. Then, with one fierce movement, the bodies collide violently. They try to seize a leg, a foot, an arm. They grab one hand, twist it, seeking to immobilise the adversary. In the space of a few seconds, life comes to a standstill, time suspends its course. They pause, recover their breath and with it, their strength. Suddenly, like a flash, a *pahalwan* is airborne and crashes on the pit. Will he succeed in untangling all these intertwined limbs that form nothing else than one body? Will he be able to pin his adversary's shoulders to the ground?

The end of the wrestling session is always a remarkable moment. Without any instruction, tacitly, everybody

The *pahalwans* share a unique camaraderie as they gather for a bath after training and prepare their favourite *badam* (almond) milk beverage.

understands that the time is over. Some gather the gears, or clean them, while others splash bucketfuls of water on each other – that has been drawn from the water well – in a playful manner, sharing camaraderie. Then they dress up and return to their activities and jobs. They never leave the *akharas* without greeting the Guruji by touching his feet.

The practice of *kushti* is widespread in north India, and especially popular in Banaras. Between 1860 and 1947, the year of India's independence, the sport was largely sponsored by the rajas. Now, the practising wrestlers themselves or former wrestlers sponsor the *akharas*. They are also helped by some generous benefactors who are passionate about the sport. But *akharas*, which in the past were numerous here, are closing their doors rapidly. While some *akharas* are transformed into more modern body-building clubs, many of them have to shut down because the discipline and the ethics that the practice of *kushti* requires are too constraining. Like many Indian institutions, *kushti* is facing many difficulties to preserve its place in the modern world.

We visited various *akharas*, some of them still in activity, some; beautiful, and some; spacious; but the one that moved us the most was the first one: Gaya Seth.

One early morning of June 2005, a friend took us to the Gaya Seth *akhara*. Only those connected with it are aware of its location; otherwise it is difficult to find amidst the winding lanes of Banaras. The first vision of the place dazed us and we were totally conquered. On our very first visit, the sadhu who used to inhabit this *akhara*, Baba Biru Das, a short, kind man with a thin body, a gentle face and penetrating eyes, invited us to come back and to continue our work. And to us, the appeal of this *akhara* was big, the desire of these encounters intense.

The first time, our Indian friend had acted as interpreter since no one in Gaya Seth knew English. But when we returned in October, speaking in Hindi increasingly became an inexorable task for us. It was time to start learning Hindi not just to facilitate communication but also because speaking the language would help us grasp the essence of what was being said.

First we communicated through gestures, then, slowly, Hindi came alive in our conversations. Seeing the effort we were making to adapt ourselves to their tongue, the wrestlers and particularly Guruji Manohar Pahalwan accepted us among them in a very friendly way.

In Gaya Seth, a very male place, the fact that we were two foreign women was never raised. Of course, it was very important to maintain some decorum and respect their privacy. Yet, at the beginning we did not realize how our presence was incongruous. Our Indian friends with whom we spoke about our project were astonished. Gradually, we understood the reason when we went to the other *akharas*. In some, we felt somewhat disrespected, especially as non-Indian women. These wrestlers neither valued themselves as wrestlers nor did they respect the beautiful tradition of *kushti's* purity. We were disappointed by some of the more famous *akharas*. In the end, the respect and kindness of the Gaya Seth wrestlers prevailed. And the best pictures we took were from there.

Sadly, when we returned after a few trips, Baba Biru Das was not there any more. Gesturing towards the sky, a wrestler announced that Baba Biru Das had joined the gods. The one who had treated us with hospitality in this splendid place was gone. Baba Biru Das was a *sannyasin* who never practiced *kushti*. As a guardian of the *akhara* shrines, he sanctified the place with his presence, by taking care of the shrine. At this moment, Guruji Manohar Pahalwan, the in-charge of training and discipline, informed us that following Baba Biru Das's will; the doors of this *akhara* would continue to be open for us. A few days went by and we all felt the absence of Baba Biru Das. All the wrestlers felt the loss of their venerated and beloved master and looked like abandoned children. One day, a new Baba arrived: Sri Das, a smiling man who was accepted in this *akhara* by virtue of his wisdom and devotion.

The courtyards of *akharas* serve as grounds for wrestlers warm-up exercises. Traditional forms of exercise and food habits are practiced to this day without much modification, despite several years of *kushti's* existence in India.

There does not seem to be any rule to choose the Baba for an *akhara*. In Gaya Seth, Manohar Pahalwan chose Sri Das as the new Baba because he knew him.

Nagapanchami is an auspicious festival in Banaras. Here, arrangements are being made under Gaya Seth's watchful eye. The *akhara* is named after him as he was the guru of the present guru and founder of the *akhara*, Manohar Pahalwan.

But it is possible that he only suggested his name and the final decision was taken by a committee. Baba Sri Das, like many Banarsis was interested in *kushti*, but he never practised it.

Time went by and we came back to this place again and again: our presence there becoming a must for us. In the middle of the perspiring atmosphere, with bodies that clashed powerfully, we attended the trainings under the pale light of the Indian early mornings. Life again took its course, imperturbably as the Ganges that flows along. We captured these rare moments on film, while the bodies intertwined with power and sensuality, softness and brutal force. It was this paradoxical bond between strength and sensuality that directed our steps here time and again.

We often stayed there after the training to watch the activities that followed. Some *pahalwans* used to get busy with the preparation of their favourite beverage: a thick blend of milk, sugar and almonds. They crushed the dried fruits into a paste on a beautifully carved ancient stone, mixed it with milk and then strained it through a cloth. The yellowish concoction would be drunk with delight. Others drew in big buckets of water from the traditional well and splashed it on each other, letting streams of muck trickle down their bodies. They even teased each other after the exertion and exhaustion.

During relaxation time, a rare kind of intimacy would be shared between the young *pahalwans* and Guruji. Some of them softened a part of the pit, around the size of Guruji, in a rectangular shape. Then they made it thicker like a 'cushion of earth' for the master to lie down. The wrestlers surrounded and massaged with infinite precaution the body of the former *pahalwan* that had suffered for so long. It was a homage of recognition and respect towards the master. This was the moment when Guruji and the disciples engaged in a real communication. Guruji would start to speak and all would listen with respect and affection, soaking in each word. It was difficult for us to understand everything he said but it appeared that Guruji was imparting lessons about life, morals and ethics. But the young wrestlers hung on to his words as if he were telling fascinating stories. The *pahalwans* seemed moved, astonished and interested. They also laughed a lot.

It was the moment of grace par excellence – an immense present they offered us by extending the privilege to witness it time and again. Sometimes, Manohar Pahalwan sang bathed in a yellow beam of light. The birds on the branches of the large banyan answered him in perfect, magical harmony.

Then, gradually, the *akhara* would become empty. Only Baba Sri Das would remain, sitting in a lotus position below the Lord Hanuman idol, a prayer book in one hand, a small bell in the other. Some neighbours, old people and children would also enter the *akhara* to worship the monkey-god, the Shiva-lingam, the banyan or simply to enjoy the freshness of the well and the shade given by the majestic branches of the 'lord of the place', the banyan.

A time comes when the wrestlers have to confront other *pahalwans* from outside – during the *dangal* (competition). *Dangals* take place on many religious holidays like Janamashtami, Shivaratri, Holi, Diwali, Valmiki Jayanti, Nagapanchami, etc., and often coincide with regional fairs. Some *dangals* even commemorate the death anniversaries of well-known local and national leaders. *Dangals* can be organized by a committee or sponsoring institution, a group of young entrepreneurs or local traders (like grain merchants or mill owners), or by municipal leaders or local village leaders. The local branch of the Rashtriya Swayamsevak Sangh (RSS), a right-wing nationalist organization also organizes *dangals*. While we were there, a *dangal* in Banaras was organized by the Cart Driver's Union, a labour organization of transport workers.

There are many small villages around Banaras where *dangals* are held and wrestlers from all these places assemble for the contest. We attended *dangals* in Chaubeypur, Chandravati and Ramayanpur, besides Banaras.

These are extraordinary days because they turn *kushti* into a festival. Hundreds of people rush to the village where the competition is being held to watch and cheer. It's an exclusive gathering of men – their faces carved by time, their silhouettes proud, their manners gentle. Our presence does not seem to disturb the event but it surprises everyone. We are offered a shaded place to sit and given water, *chai* (tea) and pastries. After so many visits we have acquired a certain kind of popularity. People recognise and greet us respectfully. (One day, Sri Das, the Baba of Gaya Seth had even accompanied us to the village of Chandravati by rickshaw, which made an impact on the villagers.)

The temporary *akhara* is adorned with flower petals and frankincense burns in its centre and at its four corners. A small earth protuberance about ten centimetres high is also covered with *malas* (garlands) made of flowers and incense, and it is worshipped and venerated like a god's statue. A large triangular red flag is perched at the top of a long mast of bamboo; it indicates the holy character of the place. Even though this *akhara* is temporary, during the time of the *dangal* it becomes a temple.

One speech is followed by another, like often in public ceremonies in India. They honour the various sponsors, politicians, other notables and benefactors by

Offerings of flowers being made during *puja*

Puja at the River Ganges

Lighting incense on the banks of the River Ganges

covering them with many garlands until their faces are entirely immersed in colour. These rituals are called *swagat* (honorific welcome). Then comes the moment of the traditional handing-over of the *gamcha*, the fabric that is used as a turban. We are also honoured in the same way several times. All this happens both before and between the matches. First, the children wrestle, then the matches gradually become more serious, long, intense and the prizes increase. The exercises are adapted to the age and the capacities of younger wrestlers. They rarely incur grave wounds. Often, they are used as sparing partners for older wrestlers and the initiation into the tougher zone is progressive.

Although one *pahalwan* from Gaya Seth won a *dangal* in Banaras, as it is one of the advanced *akharas*, the Banaras wrestlers are not systematically the best. *Akharas* from the

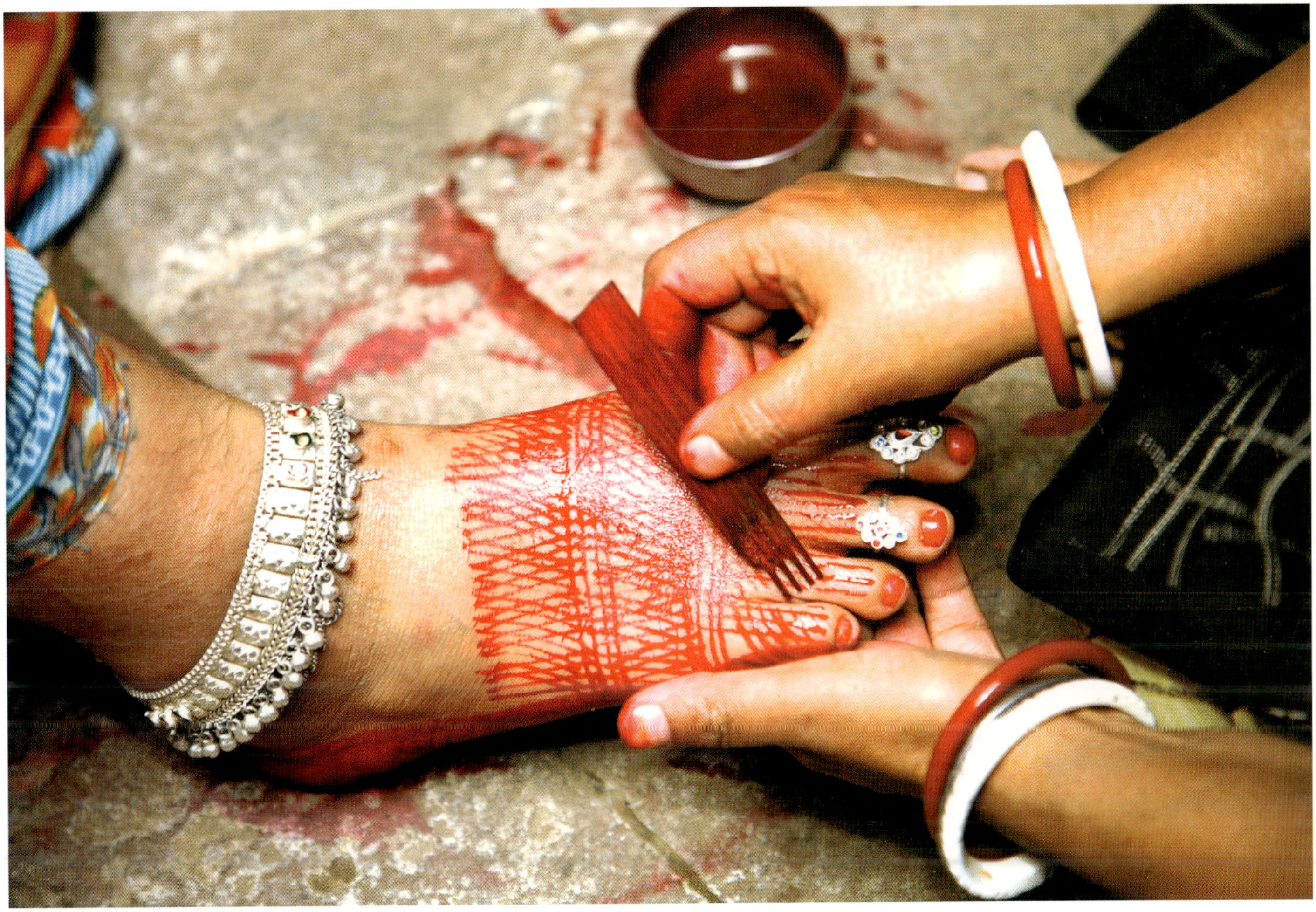

Ritual foot painting before the *puja*

villages too have talented wrestlers, who have a very high level of power and skill.

Usually, the cash prizes are of Rs 50 for the younger wrestlers, and from Rs 1,000 to 10,000 for the best wrestlers in accordance with their skill and status. Besides the cash awards, T-shirts, drinking glasses, buckets, clocks, *gamcha*, and various other items are also distributed. By nightfall, all is over and it's time for everyone to return home.

Many *dangals* are organized during the festival of Nagapanchami – celebrated during monsoon on the fifth day following the full moon that opens the month of Shravan (July-August) – within the Banaras *akharas*. Nagapanchami *dangals* are special, different from the more common, non-religious tournaments. For most Indians, this festival is dedicated to snakes, but for wrestlers, it has a

Puja at the Dashashvamedh ghat

Hands of a bride and a groom at a marriage ceremony

very specific meaning. During Nagapanchami, wrestling is an act of paying respect to Lord Shiva, Rama and Hanuman respectively by showcasing how a wrestler has developed over the year gone by. It is important here to imagine the strong heat and humidity at this time of the year, which is almost unbearable.

A few days before the beginning of the festival, the *akhara* is cleaned and totally repainted. All the paintings and drawings decorating the walls are erased and redone. The surface of the pit is levelled or changed. All the gear for training, like *gadas* and *joris*, are rinsed and purified with water, and orange swastikas are redrawn. The statues are also repainted and they shine with a new gleam. Garlands made with paper and the leaves of *neem* (*Indian lilac*) decorate the enclosing walls and the surface of the *akhara* is marked with lines to form squares. And so, the *akhara* is ready for the festival.

Starting early morning, people rush to the *akhara*. Young and former wrestlers meet each other again enthusiastically. The most awaited moment is that of the *puja*, the religious ceremony. Only the Guruji and a priest can officiate it. In Gaya Seth, where we had the immense honour to attend the ceremonies of Nagapanchami, Manohar Pahalwan was dressed in a dhoti, sitting in lotus position, directly on the pit in front of the statue of Lord Hanuman and the garlanded portrait of his own guru Gaya Seth – who was the one to name the *akhara*. Solemnly, he represented all the *pahalwans*. A fire was lit on the ground and ghee was poured on it; the priest recited mantras in Sanskrit. Incense burned around the fire and all around the *akhara*; it embalmed the entire place. *Prasad* (offerings), flowers, coins, sweet pellets were buried in the four corners and also in the centre of the pit. Then, encircling the ground amidst a dense and suffocating smoke, all the wrestlers with hands joined in front of their chest, gathered with the priest and the Guruji to pay this homage to the gods, to this ground of suffering, to this ground of battle, to this space out of time and indifferent to earthly matters. The end of this ceremony marked the beginning of the *dangal.*

An external platform had been constructed next to the *akhara,* barely a few metres from the fury of noisy rickshaws, motorbikes, buses and trucks. The traditional speeches took place, and the flowers and *gamchas* were gifted. Under the view of hundreds of people who had come from the neighbourhood and from the slums around it, the combats were launched. From their seats, the bus passengers and truck drivers too observed the fierce combats the young *pahalwans* were involved in. Food was served and the celebration began.

This *akhara* receives Muslim dignitaries with the same honours given to notables and politicians. Unlike some other *akharas,* where *kushti* is closely related to Hindu nationalist movements, Gaya Seth seems to avoid nationalist and religious discriminations. This aspect makes it outstanding and had attracted our respect.

Very often, it was difficult for Indians to believe that we were researching on *kushti* and that we used to visit the *akharas;* because it is a world of its own where two women, that too Western, cannot find a place easily. But ours was a fascinating experience; we will keep in our memory the images of entangled bodies, these painful but proud faces, the infinite kindness, and the aching limbs being massaged in a rare intimacy after the training.

We want to share all these memories because it is not certain that *kushti* will last for a long time. The iron discipline and morals values associated with it are often unimaginable for young Indians. *Akharas* were counted by the hundreds in the past but nowadays, according to an article in *The Times of India,* there are only two dozen *akharas* really practising *kushti* in Banaras. Upon visiting several *akharas* in Banaras, it comes to sight that body building and weight lifting is practiced in greater numbers, in comparison to traditional *kushti.* To encourage this sport, the Indian government is offering secure Government jobs to many wrestlers, particularly in the railways. The best *akharas* in Banaras are Gaya Seth, DLW (Diesel Locomotive Works), Ram Singh *akhara,* and Bara Ganesh *akhara.* In our opinion, Gaya Seth *akhara* rigorougly trained its people and instilled in them a deep understanding of the traditional values of *kushti.*

Even today, wrestlers are much respected and admired and most people know the names of former champions. The wrestlers habitually address each other as 'pahalwan' and the most famous ones give up their surname and gain the honour to be named Pahalwan. Very few of them definitively leave *kushti* even if they stop practising it.

At the time of our last visit to Gaya Seth, we learned that our *pahalwans* were not only the champions of Banaras, but also gold and silver medal winners in the last national championship (2007). It was impossible to get more information about this championship attended by all of them, because one of the most beautiful values of *kushti* is humility. So, we could not learn anything more about it, but we will preserve in the depths of our mind these images that belong to another time, the lessons of life embodied in the practice of Indian wrestling and the discipline that it demands. These rare and splendid moments are a gift offered to us by India, particularly by Banaras.

A sadhu after taking a ritual bath in the Ganges. He is a *muni* who has vowed to remain silent for twelve years.

Facing page: Rife with paradoxes, Banaras is a beautiful city. A man is praying near Panchaganga ghat. In the background stands the beautiful Alamgir mosque built by the Mughal emperor Aurangzeb in AD 1673.

An old man practising yoga at Shiva temple at Ahilyabai ghat. Wrestling exercises are similar to yoga, especially the *suryanamaskara* (sun salutation). Both activities are an interplay of callisthenics and breathing control.

Facing page: Two sadhus on a *ghat* smoking a *chillum*. The consumption of hashish is common among them. Although hashish consumption is prohibited in India, sadhus believe that Lord Shiva supposedly smoked hashish to tear off the veil of *maya* (illusion).

A wrestler stretches himself to his limits during exercise.

Facing page: Wrestlers warming up at the *akhara*, the ground still moist by the monsoon rains.

Wrestlers call their different exercises, *dands* and *baithaks*. These bring the wrestler, in the same way as the recitations of mantras, to a particular state of consciousness which enables inner reflection and spiritual purification.

Facing page: Force and concentration are the two most important requisites for wrestlers. In a face-to-face combat, they hold each other in total immobility, but that is followed by an attack fast as a flash.

Wrestlers help and oversee each other; here, a wrestler holds another's legs to enhance his body's flexibility.

A wrestler doing push-ups with another watching him in the mirror.

Contact with the ground is very significant. Earth is regarded as the life-giving mother, protective as well as salutary. From head to feet, wrestlers cover their body with earth.

Guru of the Gaya Seth *akhara*, Manohar Pahalwan with a wrestler, explaining a hold to him. Former champion and famous coach, he is respected across the world of Indian wrestling.

A wrestler strains with *joris* (heavy clubs used for training) but smiles with contentment. The *joris* have a swastika each painted on them, symbolising good luck and welfare.

Facing page: Wrestlers stand in the courtyard with weights, relaxing between their warm-ups, before they start wrestling.

Weight-lifting is key in daily exercises. This wrestler lifts up a *nal*, an extremely heavy stone, to develop his muscles.

A wrestler swinging a *gada*; this practice strengthens the shoulders and arms.

A wrestler performing warm up exercises with a long heavy bar weight made of wood.

A *gada* is the mark of a wrestler's prowess. In the Ramayana and the Mahabharata, it is mostly mentioned as a weapon. Lord Hanuman is usually represented with a *gada* in his left hand, signifying the destruction of evil.

A sadhu with the trademark black *tilak* of members of the Aghori sect. Devotees of Lord Shiva, this sect is believed to have split from the Kapalika order of Hinduism in the 14th century.

Facing page: A woman on the bank of the Ganges during the Dala Chhat festival, a prayer ritual followed in Bihar during Diwali.

A duel begins on the pit under the mighty Lord Hanuman's statue. Lord Hanuman is a model of power and agility. He is the warrior par excellence: immortal, tireless, and strong beyond compare. He is also capable of fervent and absolute devotion. In essence, he is all-powerful.

Pain and perspiration are the ransom to be paid for the rise of the spirit in order to be as mighty as Lord Hanuman.

Wrestling embodies the paradox of force and protection; strength through non-violence.

During *dangals* and practice sessions, each one tries to pin his opponent to the ground.

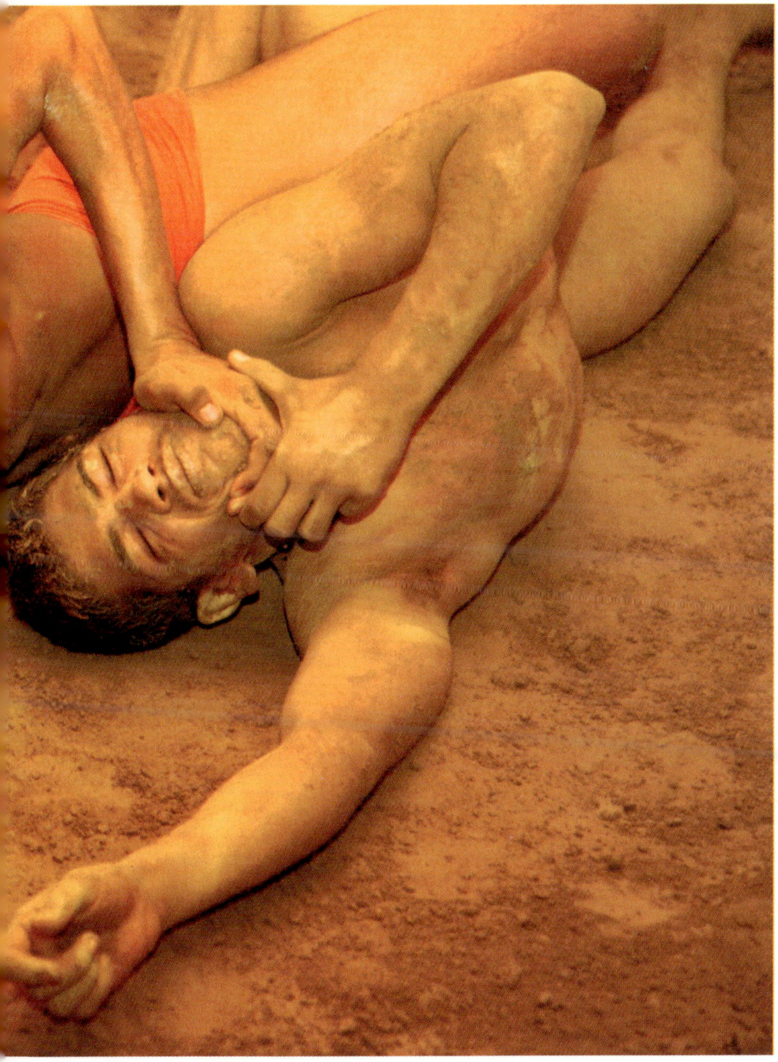

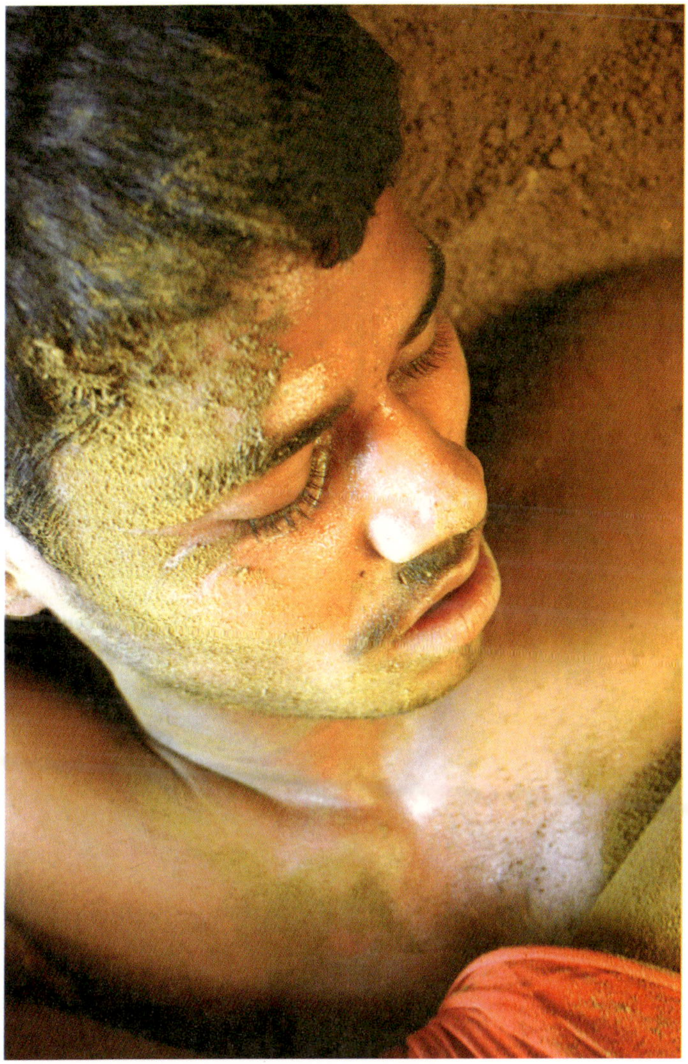

The *pahalwans'* contact with the ground is an important aspect of *kushti*.

श्री
राम

Earth, perspiration and sometimes, blood. Indian wrestling is a kind of primeval fight which involves muscular strength.

Facing page: After the match, players seek the advice of their guru. The values of respect and obedience are of utmost importance in *kushti*.

In Sant Ram *akhara* near Manikarnika, two *joris* lay beside a Hanuman statue.

Facing page: Most wrestlers have to retire by the age of thirty, but their attachment to the *akhara* is everlasting. If they don't become a coach or a referee, they keep returning to watch young wrestlers, or lift up their forgotten weights, or talk to old friends, or even to worship.

A crowded day at the Dashashvamedh ghat.

Facing page: An early morning on the Ganges in front of Ahilyabai ghat, with pilgrims feeding seagulls.

अहिल्याबाई घाट
AHILYABAI GHAT

A game of balance and power, where the body becomes a tool to fight and push a wrestler to his ultimate limits. Wrestling is the union of the mind and the body.

Movement, flexibility and power. The limbs dislocate themselves. Exaltation of the bodies and the spirit alike.

Their bodies covered with sweat and earth.

Facing page: Wrestling is a sport that lingers between softness and power. Practice sessions of three to four hours every morning and evening strengthens their minds and bodies.

Wrestlers with the *akhara's* sadhu, Biru Das in the background.

Facing page: Their bodies are hustled and stretched, but they do not break.

One of the most privileged moments of the session; after having educated the bodies, the guru 'nourishes' the spirit of the young wrestlers. Despite their aching bodies, wrestlers listen with interest and awe.

Facing page: After the training, the wrestlers surround their guru, Manohar Pahalwan, for a session of massage, teaching and relaxation. The guru occupies the pivotal place in an *akhara*. He is venerated, listened to, and more than a sports trainer, he is a spiritual guide. The wrestlers are his disciples.

The young man in charge prepares *badam* milk, while others wash themselves before returning to family or work. Water of the well of the *akharas* is famous for its medicinal value, said to cure constipation, skin infections, backaches, bruises and strain.

The method of filtering the milk mixed with sugar and crushed almonds.

A wrestler crushes almonds, the most essential ingredients used in the preparation of *badam* milk.

It is the favourite drink of wrestlers who mainly (around fifty per cent) belong to the milkmen (Yadav) caste. This popular beverage is particularly energising.

A wrestler taking a bath after training.

Facing page: Wrestlers resting in the *akhara* after training.

Two respected former wrestlers (also brothers) are reflected in the mirror of Ram Singh *akhara*.

These two brothers have been coming to their *akhara* for many years after having left wrestling. Most wrestlers' ears are torn and lacerated by years of practice, but they take pride in it. It is a *pahalwan's* prized trophy.

A customer in Gilmit Pahalwan's *chai* shop sitting under the portraits of older wrestlers. A former wrestler from Sant Ram *akhara*, Gilmit's chai shop is known to be one of the most popular in town.

Bathuk Yadav, a former wrestler at his chai shop near the Vishvanath temple. Many retired wrestlers run tea shops, where customers come to chat with the *pahalwan*.

A geometrical figure called *yantra* (tool), made with flowers, on Munshi ghat. One calls upon divinity and enunciates a *mantra* while creating the design. It is considered to be very powerful and is used for meditation.

Facing page: A view of the Banaras ghats taken from the opposite bank (from Chausatthi to Dashashvamedh ghat).

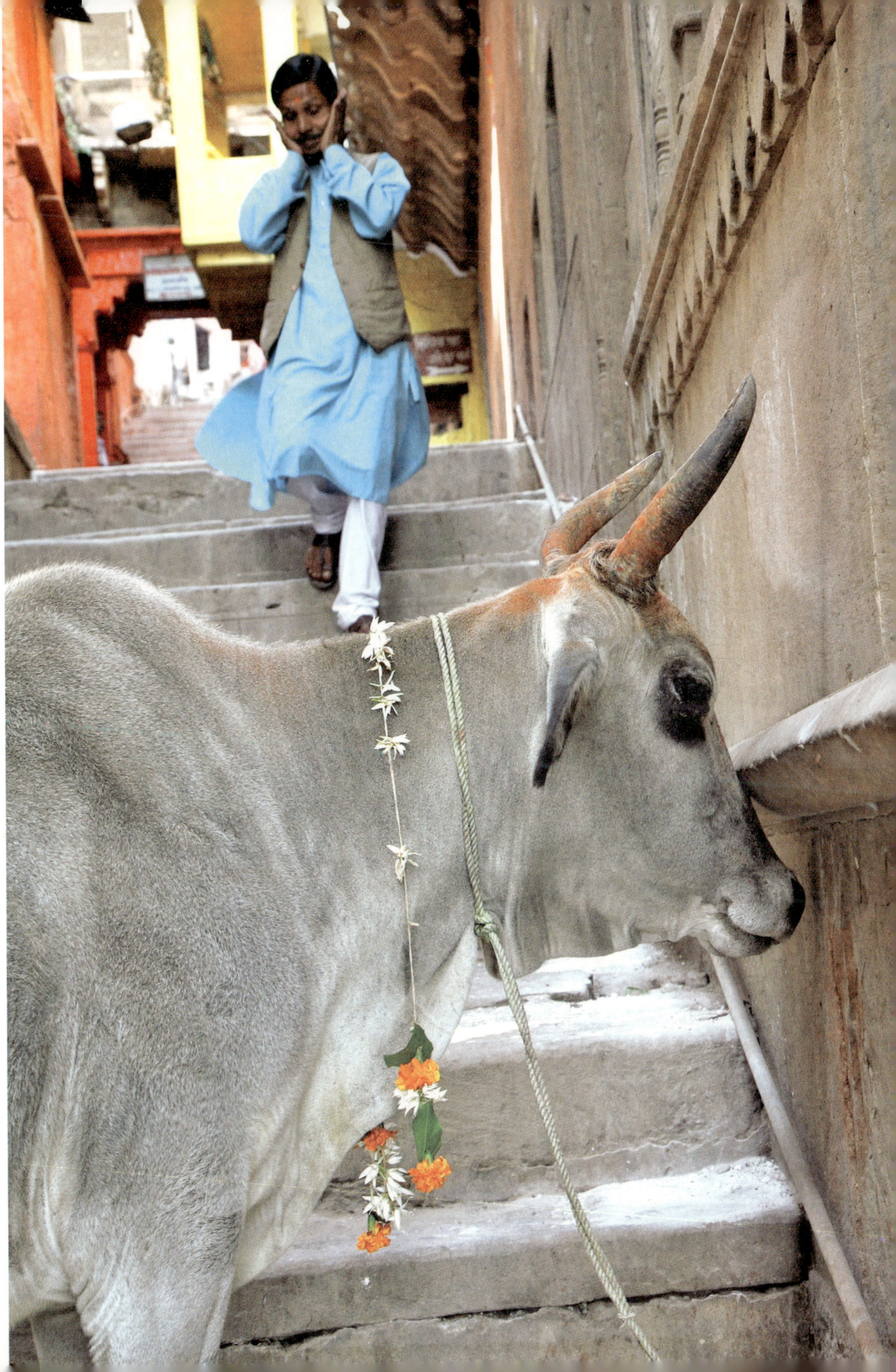

Cows are considered sacred in Hinduism. It is believed that cows provide human beings with *annada*, *vannada* and *sukhada* (food, beauty and happiness).

Facing page: A monkey plays with the *moli* (red and yellow strings used in Hindu rituals) encircling a sacred Peepal tree at Gai ghat.

अखाड़ा गुरु गया सेठ

A painter repaints the gate of the *akhara* for the Nagapanchami festival. The Hindu symbols and gods depicted are always the same: the swastika, the *om*, wrestlers, Hanuman, Shiva and Garuda (a mythical bird-like creature frequently mentioned in Hindu and Buddhist religious texts). All the mural frescos are repainted and the holy pit is decorated with garlands of leaves and sprinkled with flowers.

Preparations for the festival at Gaya Seth. Some wrestlers clean, while others paint the *akhara*. Guru Manohar Pahalwan enjoys the last few moments before the *puja* — and the subsequent competition — with his disciples.

Facing page: On the day of the Nagapanchami festival, a priest comes to perform the ritual *puja* (prayer ceremony) with the guru under the sacred image of Hanuman. All members of the *akhara* stand around the pit, as the purifying, holy fire burns.

Barbells decorated with the swastika.

Facing page: For the festival, all the training equipment is cleaned and religious symbols are repainted in an orange-red colour (the colour of Hanuman). Each disc of the weights is being painted with the swastika.

Two children along with their grandfather offering prayers under the Peepal tree in the *akhara*, which regarded as a temple; a holy place. The neighbours come to pay homage to the gods, independent of any sports activity.

Facing page: After the initial *puja*, Manohar Pahalwan proceeds to do a *puja* for the training equipment. He does an *aarti* before it with the flame burning on the plate to purify it.

Dangals (competitions) are integral to the life of villages where *kushti* is practised. Here, a dignitary who has been honoured with flowers and a turban (*mala* and *gamcha*) declares the start of the fight at a *dangal* in Ramayanpur.

Facing page: Inhabitants of the area gather at the temple grounds to watch a match.

A *dangal* taking place in Chandravati village in Uttar Pradesh. Whether combined with a religious festival or not, *dangals* provide entertainment and excitement for the villagers.

The fight starts with a play of suspicion where each wrestler measures the strength of his opponent.

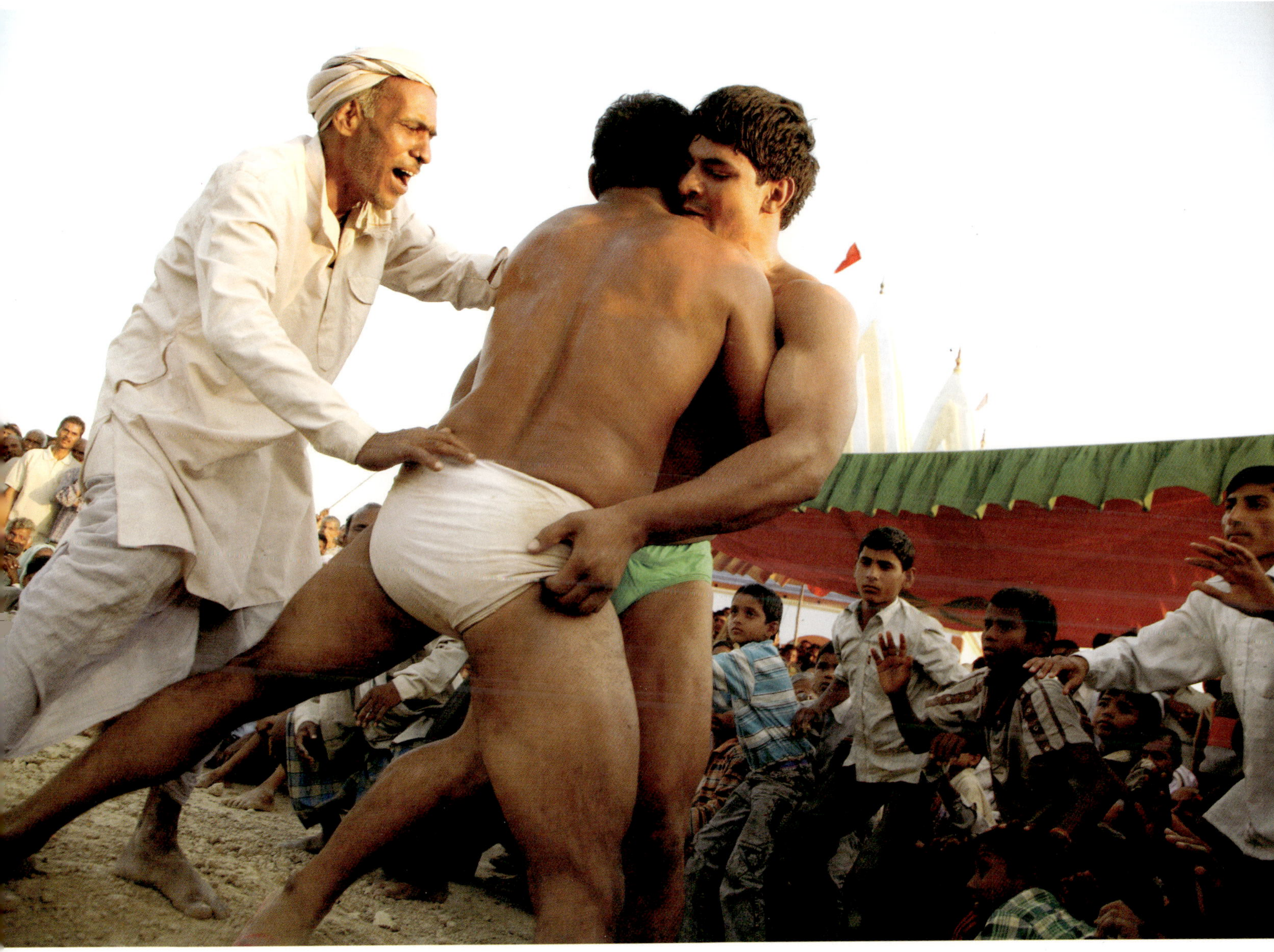

A referee intervenes during an unrelenting struggle. Wrestling is an intimate sport, where only two human bodies are pitted against each other, without any guards or gears.

A challenge taking place in a *dangal* during a festival at Gaya Seth *akhara*.

Facing page: A muddle of struggling bodies and limbs.

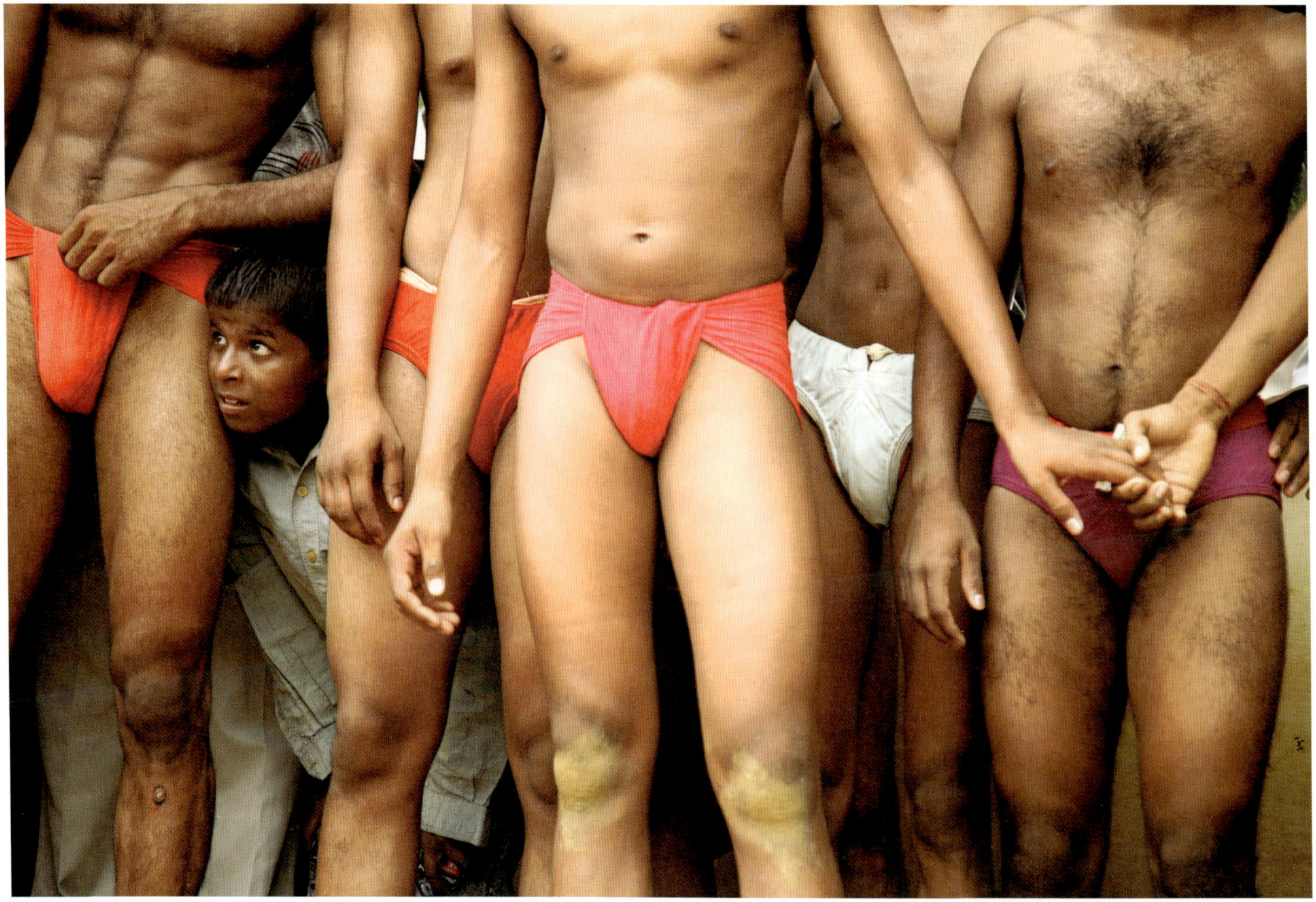

At the competition at Gaya Seth *akhara*, wrestlers are waiting to fight. The children of the area watch the wrestling championship with excitement.

Facing page: The much-awaited *dangal* takes place outside the Gaya Seth *akhara*, before the curious gaze of the bus passengers and inhabitants of the area.

The trick is to take on the opponent before he can find his bearings.

Just as Lord Hanuman is believed to fly through space, the wrestlers also enjoy playing with gravity.

The referee declares the winner of the match.

A *dangal* in Asi ghat. Manohar Pahalwan with his disciple, Rajesh Kumar, Banaras champion. Rajesh proudly carries his trophy, a golden *gada*.

ACKNOWLEDGEMENTS

- We would firstly like to thank late Baba Biru Das, who introduced us to the Gaya Seth Akhara's doors and left without closing them, and also Guruji Manohar Pahalwan and Baba Sri Das, who were always kind and pleasing, and especially all the *pahalwans* of Gaya Seth, for the respect and friendship they offered us. We would be infinitely happy if our humble book could pay all of them the homage they deserve.

- We sincerely thank the former wrestler Gilmit Pahalwan from Manikarnika for the precious information they provided us and his delicious chay.

- Our wholehearted thanks goes towards the Varanasi Rest-House in Pandey ghat who welcome us so kindly each time we visit Banaras. We also would like to warmly thank the Mukherjee family, owners of the Varanasi Rest-House.

- We extend our warmest thanks for the support and trust of Pramod Kapoor and Priya Kapoor.

- We also thank Aditi Ghosh and Richa Burman for editing the text with care and making the process so smooth.

- Thanks to Tapash and Vishvanath Biswas and their family.

- Thanks to Timsal Masud for his Urdu translations.

- I, Séverine Dabadie, would also like to thank Jacques Sinsou, who gave me so much valuable advice when I started photography long time ago and fed my love for the photography.

Facing page: A Lord Hanuman statue smeared with orange vermillion paste.

Published in India by Roli Books
M-75 Greater Kailash-II Market
New Delhi-110048, India.
Phone: ++91-11-4068 2000
Fax: ++ 91-11-2921 7185
Email: info@rolibooks.com
Website: www.rolibooks.com

ISBN: 978-81-7436-694-8

Editors: Aditi Ghosh & Richa Burman
Design: Heema Sabharwal

Printed and bound in India by
Nutech Print Services, Faridabad